PRAISE HIM WITH THE TIMBREL AND DANCE

PRAISE DANCE 101

Letricia Loftin Russell

ISBN: 9781670926845
Imprint: Independently published

DEDICATED TO...

Nina Wells, the one who awakened the writer in me and realized that I had books in my belly.

Brian Robertson, the one who awakened my sleeping drive to walk out my dreams.

My Daughters, Brianna, Brooklyne and Braxton, and Husband, Art, the ones who constantly awaken my need to achieve more.

My Lord and Savior Jesus Christ, the one who literally created and awakened me...

CONTENTS

"I have never seen praise dancing like that!"

Tye Tribbett, Gospel Recording Artist

"You girls are bad!"

Regina Belle, R&B Recording Artist

"I'm looking for your opinion… (hands us his CD promo). Do you think praise dancers will dance off of this?

James Fortune, Gospel Recording Artist

"YOU ALL ARE FABULOUS!"

Cathy Hughes, Owner/Chairman
Radio-One. TV One. Urban One

"You guys are the Alvin Ailey of praise dance!"

Pastor Mark Vereen
Hope Christian Ministries

"You have definitely found your gift to the world!"

Linda Forem, Former Vice President
Radio-One Richmond

1 THIS IS MY STORY.
   THIS IS MY SONG.

"Trish, I need you to sit down. We just had a meeting and one of our main topics of discussion was, uhhhhhh… (sighing deeply)… (blank face/lack of expression)… YOU. I know you believe that they are your friends but Honey the things that were insinuated in that meeting didn't send off the smell of support at all. If anything, totally the opposite."

Dismayed, I turn my head, blinked my eyes hard a few times, and pushed out…, "Whatttttt… who… what are you talking about"?

On this day, I learned the hard lesson again, that everyone who smiles in your face does not a friend make. Yes, they say all the right things to you in your presence, but Honey-Chile, when the doors close, when that phone disconnects, when that back is turned… what da world?!? Okkkkkk God, not again, NOTTTTTTT again. C'mon Tricia!!! How many times do you have to be stabbed before you learn to guard your heart and your real stories. Every person that offers to pray for you does not desire goodness! It seems more times than not, they actually just want to know your business to use it as their topic of "today's chatter"!!

A place that meant the world to me. A place where I spent most of my time, my talent, my everything. A place that housed most of my friends and all of my refuge turned in my place of "hell" within it

"

seems, five minutes. How could my life change so rapidly and so completely… and why did it hurt so, so bad?

Most could go home to their sanctuary in such a time as this.. Not me. That place, was the place, that forced me to this place, that ended up hurting me more than the original place. Get it???? I, uh… needed rest. I needed peace. I needed… (crying)… I didn't know what I needed!

What I did know is that I couldn't feel this hurt anymore. I couldn't bear not one more phone call scolding me about being a woman of God and needing to trust God… not one more fake hug that included a whisper telling me not to be selfish and to think about my children… not one more look of disappointment because I didn't actually match up to that "family on the church funeral fan" that so many compared us to.

I was tired of snotting (I don't "do" bodily fluids). I was tired of wiping. I was tired of hiding, fake smiling, dying inside, trying to make everyone else feel better, crying… crying… crying… it felt as easy as breathing because it's all I desired to do… and it felt I HAD NO ONE TO embrace, hug, listen, love MEEEEE!… not judge, but love ME! Was that too much to ask??

Yes, I has three amazingggggggggg daughters who loved me like… hmmmmmm… I can't think of an analogy strong enough to explain the mutual love we shared… but of course, they had not a clue what was going on in Mommy's world, cause you see… Mommy learned how to hid her dirty laundry so well that not even her children knew… and the only person she could blame was herself! Me, the only who hid everything. Me, the one that answered when asked, "Oh, everything is greattt!" Me, the one who faked it until she could make it. And now me, the one that felt as if she would rather have a nervous breakdown, an aneurysm, or even fatal car crash than continue this daily day-in-and-day-out misery! Yes, I wanted to DIE!

The times when I was driving that I thought about swerving off the road to make it look like an accident, because of course I couldn't have my girls thinking that their mother killed herself. That would kill them. Also, who would raise them? The job was assigned to me. But how God? Plus I needed to go to heaven. I had enough hell!

Like it wasn't chaotic enough, the craziness was compounded with demeaning emails sent to clergy, deacons, friends and even phone calls made to those that I loved, and believe it or not… the emails and calls were answered and concluded all with the sentencing verdict that I… Tricia… was a monster. Tricia was at fault. Tricia was in need of prayer and supplication.

Oh most certainly, I needed the latter. I needed prayer and supplication to keep me from rocking in a white room with a stray-jacket wrapped around my 5'2", 100 lb. body… or locked in a flipped upside down car burning at the bottom of a cliff in a secluded part of Henrico… or laying lifeless on a bed with an empty pill bottle balancing at the tip of my open hand. Prayer and supplication? Yep!! I needed it sure nuff!!, but not the way everyone else envisioned it.

Wowwwwwww! How is this so?! A person that almost everyone admitted had a shady side, was now the "voice" that everyone now believed and embraced as "the victim" of mean ole' Tricia! Wasn't the fact that those emails were sent, and calls were made at least a slight confirmation that I was in a negative environment? Couldn't anyone see that… even slightly? Apparently not, because each call and contact chastised me time and time and time and time and time and time and time and time and time (whew) and time again, to fix it. Forgive. Move Forward and wait for God to deliver no matter how broken and spent you are.

So you talking about DANCING??? Honey, I was dancing to save my life!! Dancing for me was like oxygen… I needed it to live!

Many tell my daughters that they wish they had our anointing!! Watch what you ask for. As Pastor John P. Kee sings, "You Don't Know My Story" (That's a good song choice for praise dancing by the way, wink)… for I'm a "chick" that knows what I'm dancing about… who I'm dancing about… and who I'm dancing for!!

Pull from your stories. Pull from your deliverances. Pull from your hurts and sorrows… hopes for tomorrow… and even better, your victories and mountain highs. But sho 'nuff, PULLLLLL!!!! Ministry is exactly that, and you can't be effective without making it personal. Now let's go to class…

Ummm, hold on just a second…

For those of you wanting to know the end of my story… well it's still being written, but let me tell you this…
Each day, I got stronger…
Each day, I got wiser…

Each day, I got better... (c'mon Marvin Sapp)!!

I promise, I am not even sure how it exactly happened. I just know I lived day to day... pressing, crying, climbing, stressing... and laying prostate on several occasions begging God to:

Be that friend to the friendless...

That comfort in the time of the storm...

And you know Saints, He did that!!! He did it suddenly, expeditiously and completely!! You know how you recognize out of the clear blue that you're "missing" that headache? I looked up one day to realize that I was "missing that heartache! God was slick with it, smile. He kindly healed and removed it, like the gentleman that He is!!

My grandmother, lovingly, tells me all the time, "Trish, you're just so happy!" And my dad teases me that, "Girl, you could be standing in the middle of a fire and you would be happy"! And even on the negative side, I overhear people say, "She is so fake. She cannot be that happy". And you know what? Positive or negative, I love when they say that. That is the "walk" that I prayed for! My answer? "You are absolutely right!!! The God I serve is worthy to be praise yall!!! I had my season of walking around hoping to die. The season of wanting everyone's validation and approval. I am completely grateful for now knowing the best response to foolishness is quietness (Thank you T.D. Jakes). And don't you see that deliverance right there?! Me, the same one who would have banged my head against the wall to make someone like me. Me, the one who constantly wanted to prove that I was a nice person now smiles joyfully when I hear or learn of a nay-sayer. It's routine proof that God is a deliverer, and that I passed the test (at least that one, smile)! I pleaded for deliverance and God did that as the young people say)!

I will not offend my God by sulking, whining, complaining and pouting. No, I am not going to make the past mistake of hiding hurts and tribulation, but I will walk, stand, and rest on the fact that my God can move mountains! I now know how to allow my tests to strengthen my testimonies... and my messes to enhance my message! I know now that like the favor of Joseph, no matter how the people try to STOP you, when you hold on to His hand, God's GOT you! Gloryyyyyyyyy!

You see, I don't need Adam, Daniel, Job, Jonah, Joseph, Abraham, Sarah, Ruth or even Mary to necessarily tell their stories. I know for myself my God is a:

Miracle Worker (c'mon now…)
Healer of Physical, Mental and Emotional Strife (and I know this to
be true)…
Comforter (I know this well too)…
Provider (yes, Sis, yes Sir)…
Fixer (waving my hands)…
Deliverer (up on my feet)…
Rewarder (screaming right now!!)

Ok, ok. I'm about to run now!!! Who wouldn't serve a God like
that?, and better yet, who wouldn't PRAISE HIM with their whole
being??

So, what are you waiting for? Let's dance y'all…

2   IT'S ALL ABOUT THE PRAISE!

dance

[dans, dahns]

verb (used without object), **danced, danc·ing.**
to move one's feet or body, or both, rhythmically in
a pattern of steps, especially to the accompaniment of music.
to leap, skip, etc., as from excitement or emotion; move nimbly or quickly:*to dance with joy.*

Wowwwwwww! How we love to dance! And to be able to do it unto God… what and HONOR! What a gift from HIM! To take the talent of movement, the strong kick of a leg… the twist of the head… the curtsy of the body… the swirl of an arm… the freedom is (might I say) priceless! We thank God for recognizing centuries ago that, we, His people could praise Him in all forms, for Psalms 149:3 states it plain, "Let them praise His name with the Dance." Thus, the very reason we want it to be very clear that Praise dancers are not to entertain you. Dictionary.com defines entertain as such:

entertain

[en-ter-**teyn**]

verb (used with object)
to hold the attention of pleasantly or agreeably; divert; amuse.

And NO!!… attention, diversion and amusement are not our goals.

Our only intention is to praise our Lord above while reminding His people of His amazing love for them. Let's take a closer look at this particular assignment from Him, and how to minister to the body of Christ as Ministers of Movement versus merely Praise Dancers, first and foremost. God inhabits the praise of His people. He commands us to praise, worship Him, and lift Him up! Through dance, we are responding to what He would have us do through movement. Our dance movement is all about praising the Lord; about being obedient to Him and his request for praise and worship. It's MINISTRY!

As dancers, we should be honored. Dance ushers in the power of the Holy Spiriit. It leads others to praise. While other parts of the worship ask for silence and attention, the dance portion of the service screams for participation and praise! It encourages the movement and clapping of hands, the patting of feet, twirling in the aisles, bouncing in the pews and swaying of the body. Not just from the dancers, but from the congregants. What a joy it is to Him, and to the congregation, when the worship experience is elevated through movement of praise! Dance does that! It's MINISTRY!

Even more of a blessing is how dance touches various senses. It is proven that different people are moved and affected in various ways, and **dance covers them all**! Be it sight, be it sound, be it movement; dance conquers each sense! Congregants can see the praise, hear the praise, and feel the praise through the movement and expression. There are nine postures of worship. Those posture are broken down into three parts: voice, hands and body.

Voice – singing, shouting, speaking
Hands – clapping, lifting hands, playing instruments
Body – standing bowing, dancing

What a blessing and gift from God. Dance encompasses more than half of the postures of worship! Through dance, congregants are led to sing, to clap, to lift hands, to stand, to bow, to dance and often to shout! Hallelujah! YOU WERE CREATED TO WORSHIP! WE WERE CREATED FOR THAT PURPOSE and as a dancer YOU ARE ASSIGNED TO LEAD THIS! What an honor. What an assignment. What a ministry.

So unlike the ENTERTAINMENT of a movie, a show, tv program or sporting event…

OUR DANCE has a higher calling, a higher purpose!
It touches people's hearts, hurts, needs, spirits and souls!
It is our response to GOD'S request that we worship and praise Him
And how better to so than with our WHOLESELVES!

It blesses HIS people and pleases HIM!
OUR DANCE is
MINISTRY!

Hallelujah!

3   RESPONDING TO NAY-SAYERS

Q: "What <u>are</u> they doing?"
A: "Dancing! Yes, <u>it's in the</u> Word!"

YES! THANK YOU GOD for recognizing from the very beginning that we your people need DANCE!

We need dance to release PRAISE!
We need dance to release ENERGY!
We need dance to release! Period!

For those who desire to question that thought, God has given us reference. Yes, biblegateway.com even confirms that the term and action of dance is in the Bible 20 times.

Some like to argue that in the Bible, dance is only mentioned regarding David, or that dance is just a new generation/young people "thang", but the Bible is solid and true, and the term dance is mentioned early on, near the beginning, in Exodus, the second book of the Bible. Even back then, the "women went out with tumbrels' and with dances".

Let's take a look:

Exodus 15:20
And Miriam the prophetess, the sister of Aaron, took a timbrel in her hand; and all the women went out after her with timbrels and with **dance**s.

Judges 11:34
And Jephthah came to Mizpeh unto his house, and, behold, his daughter came out to meet him with timbrels and with **dance**s: and she was his only child; beside her he had neither son nor daughter.

Judges 21:21
And see, and, behold, if the daughters of Shiloh come out to **dance** in **dance**s, then come ye out of the vineyards, and catch you every man his wife of the daughters of Shiloh, and go to the land of Benjamin.

Judges 21:23
And the children of Benjamin did so, and took them wives, according to their number, of them that **dance**d, whom they caught: and they went and returned unto their inheritance, and repaired the cities, and dwelt in them.

1 Samuel 21:11
And the servants of Achish said unto him, Is not this David the king of the land? did they not sing one to another of him in **dance**s, saying, Saul hath slain his thousands, and David his ten thousands?

1 Samuel 29:5
Is not this David, of whom they sang one to another in **dance**s, saying, Saul slew his thousands, and David his ten thousands?

2 Samuel 6:14
And David **dance**d before the Lord with all his might; and David was girded with a linen ephod.

Job 21:11
They send forth their little ones like a flock, and their children **dance**.

Psalm 149:3
Let them praise his name in the **dance**: let them sing praises unto him with the timbrel and harp.

Psalm 150:4
Praise him with the timbrel and **dance**: praise him with stringed instruments and organs.

Ecclesiastes 3:4
A time to weep, and a time to laugh; a time to mourn, and a time to **dance**;

Isaiah 13:21
But wild beasts of the desert shall lie there; and their houses shall be full of doleful creatures; and owls shall dwell there, and satyrs shall **dance** there.

Jeremiah 31:4
Again I will build thee, and thou shalt be built, O virgin of Israel: thou shalt again be adorned with thy tabrets, and shalt go forth in the **dance**s of them that make merry.

Jeremiah 31:13
Then shall the virgin rejoice in the **dance**, both young men and old together: for I will turn their mourning into joy, and will comfort them, and make them rejoice from their sorrow.

Lamentations 5:15
The joy of our heart is ceased; our **dance** is turned into mourning.

Matthew 11:17
And saying, We have piped unto you, and ye have not **dance**d; we have mourned unto you, and ye have not lamented.

Matthew 14:6
But when Herod's birthday was kept, the daughter of Herodias **dance**d before them, and pleased Herod.

Mark 6:22

And when the daughter of the said Herodias came in, and **dance**d, and pleased Herod and them that sat with him, the king said unto the damsel, Ask of me whatsoever thou wilt, and I will give it thee.

Luke 7:32

They are like unto children sitting in the marketplace, and calling one to another, and saying, We have piped unto you, and ye have not **dance**d; we have mourned to you, and ye have not wept.

4   TAKING ON THE ASSIGNMENT

I'm a little leery, but I was asked to…
And the Bible says, "I can do all things…"

Sooooo, now what?!

Now, let's pray!

Yes, seriously, THIS is a major assignment, and He promised that you CAN do all things, so it is time to go to Him for guidance and direction! Let us pray –

> *Dear Lord, I love you! God, I need you now! I thank you for loving me enough to choose me through Pastor (place name here) to lead and/or start this ministry. However, God, I really need your guidance! My ultimate desire is to uplift and edify you while offering our church a new and/or enhanced form of worship; also to offer a new opportunity to members of our congregation who you have blessed with an active praise to be given the chance to channel it, to share, it, and release it with power. Lead me to find the choreographer that you have designed for us, one to partner with me in this journey to set an atmosphere for a heightened praise. I thank you for a powerful, mighty Ministry of Dance here at (place name of church here)! May it become one that will bless this congregation in a way that only you can design. Amen.*

"CLARIFICATION, PLEASE…"
SET UP A MEETING WITH YOUR PASTOR

Request and schedule a meeting with your Pastor to gain clarity on his/her vision for this ministry.

- Does he/she desire for the dancers to minister monthly or just for special services (i.e.: Homecoming, Fall Revival, Vacation Bible School, etc.)

- Will this ministry minister in the sanctuary or just in the Fellowship Hall, church grounds during spring festivals, etc.?

- What age group does he/she have in mind for the ministry, if any yet?

- Is there a budget allotted for this ministry? If yes, or if no… what are the plans for purchasing music, garments, props and hiring a choreographer (if applicable)?

- What are his/her thoughts regarding the congregation's reactions to this new ministry? (i.e.: elder members, old-school deacons, traditional worshippers)

- How involved would he/she like to be in the launch and execution of this ministry?

- Lastly, why me?, smile What are his/her expectations of me leading this birthing of ministry?

"ATTENTION! ATTENTION!"
BUILD INTEREST and EXCITEMENT

Place an announcement in the bulletin, on the church website and/or megatron announcing an Interest Meeting for Ministers of Dance. Make this announcement at least two weeks out, to offer interested persons the opportunity to pray, ponder and prepare.

"IN THE MEANTIME"
PREPARE for the MEETING

Ask Pastor and the Fine Arts Minister or Minister of Music to attend. Have them greet and speak to the attendee, if even for the first few minutes. This shows them first-hand that this is an united front and joint venture to enhance the church worship experience.

"WOULD YOU COMPLETE THIS PLEASE?"
OBTAIN DETAILS FROM POTENTIAL MEMBERS

Have interested members to complete an application. The application should include their dance experience, dance knowledge, expertise of genres, training, etc. Who know, when overlooking the apps you may find that the jewel you are seeking is right in your congregation. Hallelujah! However, if not, the information on the apps will help you to know in which direction you need to head.

"SEEK AND YE SHALL FIND"
SEEK OUT A CHOREOGRAPHER

For those that do not have a Choreographer amongst the congregation, prayerfully seek. Contact local dance studios that offer Praise or Liturgical Dance. Keep your ear to the ground regarding powerful ministries in your area, and attend Praise Dance Services sponsored locally. Google and Yahoo are also great "friends" when seeking anything, and this is no exception. Believe me, when God placed this vision in your Pastor's spirit the plan was all laid out. God is intentional and does all things well. The Choreographer you seek will step forth. Just don't expect them to just drop out of the sky into your lap, smile. You may have to put some work in. As Mommy has always, and still says…

"Pray as if everything depends upon God,
but Act as if everything depends upon you!"

With these working together, it will work out.
Work and pray. Pray and work.
Faith without works is dead!

The Choreographer **will** come forth. Everything you need will come forth.
-or-
Choreography gifts that you didn't even know you had **will** rise forth!
It all will rise forth. Amen?
AMEN!

5   RULES? DO WE REALLY HAVE TO HAVE RULES?

Uhhhhhh… YESSSSSSSSSSSS!!!

Don't we serve a God of order?
Don't we serve a God of excellence?
YESSS!   Therefore, we must certainly outline/set-up guidelines by which to follow.
The United States of America has the Amendments.
The Church has its By-laws.
The corporate world has the Employee Handbook.
The school systems have the Student Code of Conduct.
And even your little league and neighborhood associations have Regulation Policies.

And aren't we on an assignment even more important as those aforementioned? I would say that answer is an overwhelming YES!!! We most certainly are! Now isn't that humbling? (Are you smiling yet?)

So let's just look at some rules, or should we say "Guideline Directions":

REHEARSAL ATTENDANCE and PREPARATION

Set-up a rehearsal schedule (i.e.: every Monday at 7:30 p.m. or the three Saturdays that lead to their assigned Sunday or every 2nd and 4th Tuesday evening prior to choir rehearsal).

Three rehearsals leading up to ministry day is the standard, but keep in mind your team's experience and learning curve. Design a schedule that embraces your team. Once the schedule is et, administer rules regarding attendance. Below are some suggestions:

All rehearsals leading to a ministering opportunity are mandatory. If a rehearsal has to be missed during that cycle, the dancer will serve as an intercessor (which is just as important if not more so) while her/his counterparts minister. That dancer will join the troupe formation again for the next dance ministry opportunity.

-OR-

After notifying the director of an anticipated missed practice, the dancer will meet with a fellow team dancer to learn what was taught and show up to the next practice abreast and up to par.

-ALONG WITH-

The final practice prior to the ministry date is mandatory. This is necessary to ensure that all dancers are well versed in the dance, and that they are comfortable with the formations and transitions. This leaves them free to minister without feeling unsure and insecure; to dance in strength, power, familiarity and anointing vs. second-guessing every step or move.

AN "ah–hah" MOMENT	Also, it is probably a good idea to type up a "handy-dandy" notebook or one-sheeter stating the rules and expectations. Have each dancer and parent (if applicable) sign in case of "amnesia" in the future, lol.

Other guidelines will/may include garment care, behavior and preparation. (more details to come in Chapters 5 and 10)

6   WHAT TO WEAR?
WHAT TO WEAR?

That's a woman's question everyday, right? (smile) This is definitely no exception… even more so!

So now, look at your team for direction. Direction regarding their shapes, their body sizes, the ages of your ministers, their genders, and their movement.

Be honest. How will your size 2 dancer look in the garment? How will your size 16 or 22 look in the garment? Will the dancer equipped to wear a size D bra look the same as the dancer in the training bra? Will your gentlemen still look and feel comfortable in the attire that you have selected? And on the other hand, will your female dancers feel confined like they are wearing tents or burlap bags?

Although we desire for the garments to enhance the ministry and to not entice lustful thoughts, we also don't want to push the message that dance ministers must resemble the women of the 1800s. There is a balance (smile). Find the happy medium.

Also keep in mind the amount of layers chosen to lessen the enticement. Remember that dancing is a work-out indeed! The average athlete works out in a limited amount of clothing which is intentional to free-up movement and minimize perspiration. When layering your dancers with leggings, palazzo pants, a dress or leotard, then tunic, etc, you are heightening the chance of hyperthermia, asthma attacks and heat exhaustion. Trust me! I know all too well from making this mistake with my troupe. There's nothing worse than the feeling of witnessing one or more of your ministers being cared for by church nurses or EMTs… or even worse being carried away in a siren-ing ambulance.

AN "ah-hah" MOMENT	**Consider this.** **No other minister is expected to wear that many layers and ironically, no other minister exudes nearly as much energy.**

Consider ruffles or flaps to camouflage the chest, and a jumpsuit or one-piece to keep legs covered when your dancers spin or twirl. Also keep in mind the weather, season and temperature kept in your particular place of worship.

The ultimate goal is to have the dancers in "garments of glory" but also "garments of safety and comfort".

7   OUUUU! THAT IS MY SONG!

That song is just so beautiful. It's like a lullaby. The beat of that song is so funky and hype. But is a lullaby or a funky beat the right selection for your dancers or your congregation? Everything with a melody is not designed for dance ministry.

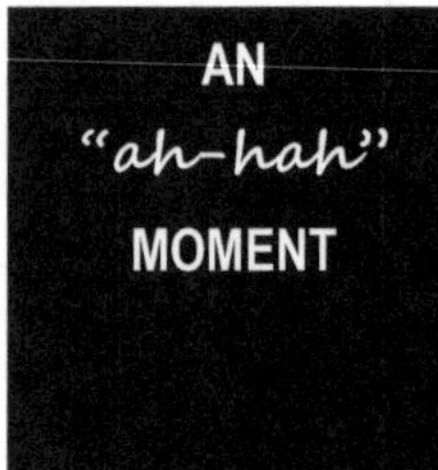

You know how they say a huge part of a business' success is *location, location, location*? Well, when ministering through dance, a huge part of the congregations' receipt is *song choice, song choice, song choice.*

Now take heed, every song that sounds good on the radio is not necessarily a good choice. Just like a Minister of Music needs to evaluate his congregation, his choir and their gifts, strengths and weaknesses prior to choosing a song to teach, a Minister of Dance needs to do the same – evaluate the congregation, the dancers and their gifts, strengths and weaknesses when selecting a song to bring forth movement.

Below are some hints when selecting a song:

THE MESSAGE IS IN THE MUSIC

Just like we spoke about earlier on, some congregants may be in a season where movement is their ministry of choice, their main form of uplift. They may be visual learners and therefore thirsty for the minutes of service when you, the dancers, come forth.

What is your message? Are you comforting them with a reminder that "The Battle is not Their's, it's the Lord's"...

Or charging them to say "Yes" and to "Give Themselves Away"...

Or celebrating with them that their "Name is Victory" and to "Praise Him in Advance"...

Or encouraging them to "Stomp" and be "Souled Out" as they "Lift Him Up" with the "Anthem of Praise"?

DOES IT CALL FOR MOVEMENT?

Does the song tell a story that the dancers can illustrate through movement?

When the Psalmist sings the phrase "my hands are made to worship you"... can you picture your dancers' movement? Does the song exude excitement to invite and encourage excitement and movement? Does the song climax? Ask your Father for guidance...

> *Heavenly Father, it's me again! I am preparing for ministry and I need you! Please speak to me regarding my song choice.. Alert me of the congregation's needs and Pastor's message points. When listening to the radio and/or -----, allow the right song to "stand out". Show me choreography and movement as the song plays. Choreography that will bring this song "to life" and will your people to a high praise and worship. I trust you! I thank you! Amen.*

-THEN-

Once you are clear on your song selection, make sure that the message is clear and in the spirit of your dance team.

HELPFUL EXERCISE
- EXERCISE A -

Have your dancers sit throughout the sanctuary… all on separate pews/rows, and then play the song. Ask them to not talk or interact, but just to listen attentively. Allow the song to minister to them.

Once the song has played, begin to ask each dancer to share what they believe the message is and how does the selection touch them personally. This should start a dialogue that helps them to truly embrace the message and should set them up to learn the choreography.

8   5-6-7-8
THE CHOREO!

Envision your sanctuary or place of worship. Use each diagram to draw in the pews, aisles, pulpit… and don't forget doors and entry ways. Also remember your balcony and far side aisles. Now sit and consider various ways that your dancers can utilize the space to best minister to your congregation. Be creative and change it up with each diagram.

Diagram 1

Diagram 2

Diagram 3

Listen to the song over and over and over again! And again! Ok, now listen again, smile. Allow the song to soak deep into your spirit! Once done, the message, the choreography, and the vision will become plain. As the vision strengthens, allow yourself to think out of the box!

Although your dance IS MINISTRY... and it is!, use the fact that it is "art" too... and allow the "art-sy side" to raise up your creativity. Think about incorporating...

Solos,
Duets,
Trios,
Shadowing,
Across the Floors,
Transitions,
Surprise Entrances,
Own Praise (Improvising),
and even
Props.

Let's take a more intimate look:

SOLOS

Inventory your group.
What style dancers have you been blessed with?
Do you have an incredibly graceful dancer?
A rhythmic tap dancer?
One who has mastered ballet or pointe?
What about Modern?
Hip Hop?
Even, Salsa!...

HINT: Yes, choose the Salsa steps wisely… but imagine the flair that would bring to the praise when done properly!!

Featured in praise dance catalog

DUETS

Do you have dancers that truly compliment each other?
Do they truly bring out the best of one another?
Or on the other hand…
Could you partner one of your stronger dancers with a "weaker" one to offer balance?
Is there a piece of the song where a duet/trio or two would fit nicely?

Troupe ministering at Virginia Union University

SHADOWING

Is there a piece of the song where the psalmist sings a line then the choir repeats? (i.e.: If so, to build on that vision that God gave the writer/psalmist, allow your dancers to do the same. Have a dancer step ahead of the dance team and to make a move to match the psalmist and then the rest of the dance team mimic the dance move with power… just as choir repeats the psalmist).

Keep the same leader throughout or for the climax-sake, switch out the dance leader for power and excitement. The key to this is for the background dancers to mimic their leaders(s) with full power and energy… and for the energy to build.

ACROSS THE FLOORS

Does your sanctuary offer a spacious area in front of the pulpit? Is there a spacious, center aisle or two centered double aisles that would offer a dancer or two the spacing to leap, barrel-turn or sa-shay as the song climaxes?

-or-

Even allow a pointe' dancer to "toe" during the beautiful interlude…
A modern dancer to cha-nay turn as the psalmist hits a 'high praise' in the song?
Utilize your space and utilize your dancers and their gifts and teachings.

31

HINT:
Some of your dancers have been taking dance classes for years. Wouldn't it be a blessing for them to share their trained gifts with the congregation? To use their training to lead praise and edify God? Plus, it would make Mommies and Daddies happy to see their investment used for the Kingdom too, lol)

SURPRISES ENTRANCES

Notice the number of entrances into your sanctuary.
Is there an entrance or two in the choir loft, the pulpit?
Midway down the side, wall aisles?
How about a balcony or even baptism pool?

Depending on the song, a dancer or two can enter from a non-traditional door. Keep your congregants guessing. Keep them excited, on the edge of their seats, and eager to build the praise experience. Even have a dancer enter and dance in the balcony. Have the dancers nod toward the balcony, or motion in that direction, or even partner with your media ministry to have the lighting match dancers' entrances.

Also remember, all dancers do not have to enter at the beginning of the presentation. Utilize the entire song and make it a "building" experience with surprises. Your congregation will welcome it!!

TRANSITIONS

Instead of your dancers routinely standing in a staggered line across the front of the church, shake it up! Surprise your congregation! Have your dancers in the aisles –
    All in the center aisle
    In various aisles throughout the church
    In the pilpit
    In the choir loft
    Throughout the sanctuary including the balcony
    And the overflow room (if applicable)

HINT:
Yes, even the worshippers watching the monitors would
love to witness/feel the experience live, smile.

Then don't feel as if the positioning has to remain the same throughout. Have your dancers switch up and elevate the praise through transitions.

"OWN" PRAISE

What is that?! Well, it's when a dancer just begins to flow freely and use their own personal choreography, on-the-spot, as the songs plays. The dancer "owns" the praise. They take ownership and it's all their own. They move however God lays on their heart.

It is great to release dancers to "own" praise during the climax of a song or even when the psalmist begins to ad-lib during the selection… in a state of "own" praise in the singing form. However, plese be sure that your dancers are gifted, anointed and trained enough to be released to "own" praise, otherwise you just end up with a bunch of dancers just kicking and waving their arms aimlessly. That would not be effective ministry, smile

PROPS

Streamers, flags, banners, oh my! You talking about a beautiful sight and setting of celebration? That beautiful sight of vibrant color swayng, twirling and pirouetting in the sanctuary is incredible!!

Why not have your dancers run in with flags or pick up streamers hidden under a pew to heighten the celebratory look and feel during the rendition.

Other props often overlooked, however just as effective – church fans, gloves, and even umbrellas and/or ponchos. Nothing takes the congregation back to the "ole time way" like church fans, church hats and white gloves -or- dancing in chairs -or- strengthening the message of asking God to "rain on Us" and "I Told the Storm" like props of umbrellas and ponchos.

HINT:
Yes, they make actual dance umbrellas that are light-weight and easy to dance with.

Whewwwwwwwwwwwwwwww!! – a lot, huh?! Yes, allow your creativity to explode. This is for God!! He deserves our very best... the HIGHEST PRAISE! No holds barred! There is no greater celebration than the love that He has for us!

Celebrate it! Celebrate HIM! Don't allow any mainstream dance team to be more creative than you! They are merely entertaining... and YOU are MINISTERING!!! Take it there!!

9 BUT WON'T I LOOK UGLY?

Exactly!
We are not models, we are not prima-ballerinas…
We are DANCE MINISTERS!

We have a message to tell through our movement… And that is impossible to do so minus facial expression!… even if it causes us to look what some may call ugly, smile.

When you desire to be effective, you use facial expressions. Don't you use facial expression when disciplining your child… when telling your spouse how much you love them… when sharing your proposal idea to your boss. Is is possible to engage a room full of people without facial expression? Have you been in a lecture when the professor and/or speaker used a monotone voice and blank faces? How long did they hold your attention and how enriching was that experience? Not very.

In the same sense, how engaged do you think your congregation will be to your dance team with them dancing with blank faces; giving off the vibe that they are bored and aloof.

Let's look to great "praisers" in the Kingdom…
Yolanda Adams
Tye Tribbett
Shirley Caesar
The Mighty Clouds of Joy
All different types, but praisers indeed… different styles, different

sounds, different audiences but same effective praise! Are they before the people singing with blank faces and "non-chalant-ness" -or- with an excitement... strong, powerful emotion that most certainly demands facial expression?!

HELPFUL EXERCISE

- EXERCISE B -

Have each dancer stand flat against a wall. Stand erect, even, with heels planted to the wall. Then turn on an emotional, moving gospel selection, and have them minister to that selection using their faces only! They are not to move any muscle in the body below the neck.

When done effectively, I promise ministry can be brought forth. Facial expression is that important... that necessary... that moving.

Make facial expression mandatory for your team. Be sure that they totally understand the message of the song (see HELPFUL EXERCISE A in Chapter 6) so that they may easily and effectively exude the message through their faces.

10 "WHAT DA WORLD?!?"

Ahhhhhhhhh! Now that the dance ministry is established and/or enhanced…
Now that it is blessing the people…
Now that the worship experience has been elevated…
You can relax, right?
Wrong! You know what's coming, right?...
Attacks!
You've heard the statement, "Ministry Costs!" It does! But there is good news!! Our God has promised…
"What shall we say to these things, If God be for you, who can be against you?" -Romans 8:31
"No weapon formed against you shall prosper." -Isaiah 54:17
Should I go on?

Keep these promises close to your breast for when you, personally, are feeling tired and overwhelmed… and for you to pour into your team when they are down-trodden.

The attacks may appear as such:

FOR THE TROUPE MINISTRY

- Some undercover dancer in the congregation may be insulted that they were not chosen to lead the troupe so they begin to nick-pick and overly critique.
- Some old-school, traditional church goers may still not want to embrace the elevation and newness of the praise experience.

They may argue that it doesn't "take all that".

FOR ADULT DANCE MINISTERS

The morning of ministry…

- One dancer's household may have a toddler wake-up with a tummy-ache, forcing the dancing mom to change focus
- Another household may have a spouse to begin to spat about an issue that they failed to even mention prior to the morning, but now they deem it pertinent to discuss immediately
- An iron may decide to stop working right when it's time to hit the wrinkles of that never-ending circle-shaped dance dress that sat laying in the dryer all night.
- When jumping in the car, it's past "E", and of course you budgeted only the perfect amount of minutes to get to the church -or- you don't have two nickels to rub together, thus reason the car is still on "E".
- The teenage daughter missed curfew last night and is walking around pouting and attitudinal due to the unfair punishment she believed you issued.

Can you say, WHAT da WORLD!?

FOR YOUTH DANCE MINISTERS

- Mom is a snappy turtle… "barking" at everyone in the house it seems because we're running behind and she doesn't want to look bad.
- The praise dance garments that are supposed to always hang in a special place in the closet, are oddly enough not there, and mom is calling from the front door that it is time to go. Oh my God, literally!
- When checking social media, a so-called friend has made a sarcastic, offensive comment under one of my posts and thousands of followers have viewed it.
- Tension in the house is so thick because parents aren't speaking to each other, however they behave totally opposite from this, and smile and act "fake" once the car pulls up to the church. It's nerve-wrecking!

So what to do? It's now 30 minutes before the Praise & Worship team takes the pulpit and most of your dancers have stumbles and slugged in… frazzled, anxious and stressed. Not to mention that you, yourself, received a distressing call on your cell just as you were pulling into the church parking lot. Of course, your non-church-going co-worker calls you panicked about tomorrow's project that is falling apart.

Soooooooooooo, now your dressing area feels tense and dark with dancer ministers that are hurt and bothered with broken spirits. Dance Ministers that certainly don't feel empowered to lead God's people in any form or fashion. How do we change this atmosphere?

Grab the phone and pump up some music. Not the selection that you all are dancing to today. That will usually cause them to want to practice or discuss moves and positions. No, right now we want t minister to their hearts and spirits. Choose a selection that is soothing and uplifting – one that reminds them to "trust God" or say "yes" to His call, or to remind them of how He loves them so much. Ask them to remain silent while they dress and ask them to allow the music to minister t them and their circumstances, so that they may be suited up to minister to their congregation.

Gather them in a chain circle where their arms are locked at the elbows and not just their hands. I learned this link-chain from ministering with the Praise Dancers of Mt. Gilead Full Gospel International Ministries. This brings you closer and makes the mood more intimate and personal. Then ask on of your "sure-nuff" gifted prayer warriors to begin to "go-in" – declaring VICTORY and calling for God to "come by there". This is a time for a "declare war". "Threshing floor" type of prayer. If you do not have a gifted, anointed prayer warrior in your troupe, run and grab Sister Hattie or Deacon Fran from the church office, vestibule or wherever. You are now charged to prepare your dancers for labor and delivery. You all have been pregnant with this message and its birthing time. Labor is not fun, in all actuality, it is painful! Each aforementioned incident that occurred in each household, and in the church house was a contraction! Breathe deeply through it! Explain this to your dancers so they, too, can recognize it and breathe deep, hard and fast. Remember, each contraction is necessary and brings you closer to a victorious birthing!

Now of course this stress won't be the case each time you stand before the people but preparation, fasting and prayer need to be continuous weapons to keep the ministry strong, healthy and growing… just like a mom caring for their newborn. There are crying times… and precious, peaceful times.

As the newborn grows to the toddler stage, school age, tween/teen road, etc. – new trials and challenges will arise – however so will new victories and successes. Trust God!

Growth is inevitable! Hallelujah!

Growth for you personally…

Growth for your dance team individually and collectively…

Growth for the praise and worship of your congregation…

God is pleased!

And as the ole gospel song chimes…

Ain't that good news?!!

Preparing to minister to thousands at Radio One's Transformation Expo

11   THE COMMITMENT.
THE CONTRACT.

This chapter co-written with Minister Hardy Lee Abbott, Jr.

God moved in the beginning even when He created the heavens and the earth. It left us with the responsibility to continue movement. That movement should have purpose behind it. Like God the Father, our movement should possess power. It should have a creative element that is able to produce.

What should it produce?
It should produce an atmosphere of liberty and worship. Movement ministry should produce a feeling of encouragement and edification (intellectual, moral or spiritual improvement; enlightment).
It should uplift broken and wounded spirits.
It should produce a spirit of anticipation.

And as you now know, it is your assignment to create and led the aforementioned. Are you willing to move… to prepare… to commit? Of course you are!

You recognize that entertainment is for the stage…
And ministry is for the people!
You have prayed, prepared, practiced…
You have asked God to appoint and anoint you for such a time as this…
You have thanked God for choosing you to serve as one of His leaders of praise…
You have bonded with, and continue to pray for your Dance Leader and fellow dance ministers.
So now…

THE PREPARATION

Before every ministry assignment I will prepare

MY PRAYER

I will continuously pray that God uses me as a vessel of Praise and Worship. I will allow the Holy Spirit to make me free to worship God so that when I am dancing, the people in the congregation won't see me; I want to decrease so that God will increase.

MY SPIRIT

I will focus on scriptures that relate to the subject matter in the song I am ministering. I will use my Bile's concordance or biblegateway.com to find scriptures that reference the song choice. Also, read and meditate on verses in the Bible that have always gotten me through… and remember to worship in spirit and in truth."

John 4:24 New International Reader's Version (NIRV)

24 God is spirit. His worshipers must worship him in the Spirit and in truth."

Colossians 1:10-11 New International Reader's Version (NIRV)

10 Then you will be able to lead a life that is worthy of the Lord. We pray that you will please him in every way. So we want you to bear fruit in every good thing you do. We pray that you will grow to know God better. 11 We want you to be very strong, in keeping with his glorious power. We want you to be patient. We pray that you will never give up.

MY TEMPLE

I will eat healthy and stay hydrated, understanding that H20 is a gift from God, smile. I will work out regularly to build up my endurance and strength. I want to minister with power and energy.

1 Corinthians 6:19 New International Version (NIV)

Do you not know that your bodies are temples of the Holy Spirit, who is in you, whom you have received from God? You are not your own;

Psalm 139:14 New International Version (NIV)

I praise you because I am fearfully and wonderfully made;
your works are wonderful, I know that full well.

ADDITIONAL COMMENTS:

Signature: ____

Date: ______________________________________

MY COMMITMENT TO THE MINISTRY OF DANCE

1. I believe Christ died for me and the sins of the world.
2. I believe that movement ministry requires 100% commitment.
3. I believe that I need to cooperate with the Director and/or Choreographer and be willing to learn.
4. I believe that it is important to support and uphold those elected and appointed to lead the ministry.
5. I believe that it is important to cooperate with decisions made by the leader and/or majority of the troupe.
6. I believe that it is important to attend all rehearsals, and will contact the Dance Leader/Minister if I am unable to attend.
7. I believe that it is important to come to rehearsals with a positive attitude towards dance ministry.
8. I believe that it is important to regularly attend all ministry engagements.
9. I believe that it is important to be punctual (early/on time) for ministry engagements.
10. I believe that it is important to peacefully express concerns to only those in authority who can bring about change.
11. I believe that movement ministry requires time, hard work, dedication and determination.

I will have fun and experience and express the joy of the Lord.

I agree to follow, live and model, the manners of movement ministry listed above.

Signature: ____

Date: ___________________________

Troupe interacting with Gospel Artist James Fortune at GMWA

Troupe opening for Dr. Jamal Bryant Tour

Troupe Opening for Gospel Comedian Marcus D. Wiley

Troupe with Gospel Icon Shirley Caesar

ABOUT THE AUTHOR

Letricia Loftin Russell is an award-winning gospel radio personality, and can be heard throughout the U.S. on her national syndicated radio show, heard in 53 cities. A graduate of Hampton University, and current candidate for her Master of Theology, Loftin is also the author of "Not to Entertain You - The Ministry of Dance". She travels the nation conducting Praise Dance Workshops and Book Signings. Her talent has allowed her praise dance mentees to open for gospel recording artists Marvin Sapp, Yolanda Adams, James Fortune, Vickie Winans and numerous other A-list gospel stars.

Loftin is the Marketing and Public Relations Coordinator of First Baptist Church of Glenarden's non-profit arm, SHABACH! Ministries. Her joy of creative ministry has allowed her to also pen a children book series and design a line of scripture based scented soy candles.

Pageantry is in her DNA. She is a pageant queen, judge, coach, director, and her favorite - pageant mom. Her daughter is the reigning Miss Hampton University. She has judged and coached for the Miss America Organization, Miss United States, and numerous others. Her ministry of pouring into young ladies landed her even blessed to launch and direct Cynthia Bailey's Miss Renaissance Pageant; even making a cameo appearance on the television show, "Real Housewives of Atlanta".

With her busy schedule of out-of-box ministry, and community service, Loftin recognizes and is grateful for her greatest gifts from above, her husband, and three adult daughters that joined her in every aspect of her dance ministry. She could not have walked out this assignment without them, their talent and love. Loftin is also a Bonus Mom of two. The love of these six clothe her daily with the promise in Psalms 23:5-6, "...thou anointest my head with oil, my cup runneth over. Surely goodness and mercy shall follow me all the days of my life."

Relaxing with Gospel Icon and Radio Host Dorinda Clark Cole
- Photo Credit: Art Russell III

Backstage with Gospel Artist and Radio Host JJ Hairston and Comedian Kasaun Wilson

-Photo Credit: Art Russell III